Introduction:

In recent surveys, over 60% of Americans say they would be willing to study the Bible if someone asked them.

If you were to study the Bible with someone, how and where would you start?

Do you have a simple method to study the Bible that anyone can use to draw out the meaning?

How would you describe what the Bible is all about?

This study is designed to help answer these questions.

These 8 Bible chapters provide an overview of the entire message of the Bible… God's redemption of broken people.

The methods we use can be applied to any Bible passage to help you understand and apply the meaning to your life.

You do not have to be a Bible teacher to lead someone in this study. Simply turn to the first session and follow the instructions.

Many blessings,
Gary & Ed

Table of Contents

Session 1	Genesis 3	Sin Enters the World	1
Session 2	Exodus 20	God Gives 10 Commandments	5
Session 3	Psalm 103	God's Loving Character	8
Session 4	Isaiah 53	Messiah Offered for Sin	11
Session 5	John 1	God's Son Comes to Us	14
Session 6	Matthew 28	Jesus' Death & Resurrection	18
Session 7	Romans 8	Victorious Christian Living	22
Session 8	Revelation 20	Jesus Returns to Rule	26
		Next Steps	29
		The Gospel of Mark	30

DEDICATION

A special note of dedication and thanks to **Ed Watson** (1943-2017), my partner in ministry, whose commitment to train disciple-makers provided the environment for learning, and applying, the principles contained in this material within the context of the American church.

–Gary Stump

Scripture quotations are taken from the Holy Bible, New Living Translation, copyright **©1996, 2004, 2007, 2013, 2015 by Tyndale House Foundation. Used by permission of Tyndale House Publishers, Inc., Carol Stream, Illinois 60188. All rights reserved.**

TRANSFORMING CHURCHES NETWORK

Transforming Churches Network
1736 Edgeburg Lane | Cordova, TN 38016
901-494-7375
www.tcnprocess.com
terry@transformingchurchesnetwork.org

Session 1 — Genesis 3 — Sin Enters the World

 These note boxes contain important information. Be sure to read each "NOTE" out loud during your time together.

- ☐ BEGIN BY PRAYING TOGETHER

- ☐ READ THIS PASSAGE TOGETHER TO FOCUS ON GOD'S CHARACTER: **Psalm 19:1–3 The heavens proclaim the glory of God. The skies display his craftsmanship. ² Day after day they continue to speak; night after night they make him known. ³ They speak without a sound or word; their voice is never heard.**

- ☐ LIST A HIGHLIGHT FROM LAST WEEK & CHALLENGE YOU ARE FACING

Highlight	Challenge
_____	_____
_____	_____

- ☐ WHO SHOULD BE A PART OF THIS BIBLE STUDY?

_____   _____

_____   _____

The Bible is the most read, revered and controversial book in the history of the world. It is estimated that there are over 6 billion copies currently in print—that is almost one for every person on planet earth. What is the reason for the popularity of this book? What are the major themes of the Bible? How can we understand what it is saying—especially for us today?

"The Bible was written between 2000BC and 100AD by 40 different human authors and yet tells one consistent story of God pursuing us to be in a right relationship with Himself. It is divided into two major parts: Old Testament and New Testament.

"We will begin from the book of beginnings, Genesis. In it we are told that God created the universe and then created the first two humans, Adam and Eve. They lived in a perfect environment that God had provided for them. Then everything changed. We read about this in Genesis chapter 3."

- ☐ READ GENESIS 3:1-24 OUT LOUD.

The serpent was the shrewdest of all the wild animals the LORD God had made. One day he asked the woman, "Did God really say you must not eat the fruit from any of the trees in the garden?" ² "Of course we may eat fruit from the trees in the garden," the woman replied. ³ "It's only the fruit from the tree in the middle of the garden

that we are not allowed to eat. God said, 'You must not eat it or even touch it; if you do, you will die.' " ⁴ "You won't die!" the serpent replied to the woman. ⁵ "God knows that your eyes will be opened as soon as you eat it, and you will be like God, knowing both good and evil."

⁶ The woman was convinced. She saw that the tree was beautiful and its fruit looked delicious, and she wanted the wisdom it would give her. So she took some of the fruit and ate it. Then she gave some to her husband, who was with her, and he ate it, too. ⁷ At that moment their eyes were opened, and they suddenly felt shame at their nakedness. So they sewed fig leaves together to cover themselves.

⁸ When the cool evening breezes were blowing, the man and his wife heard the LORD God walking about in the garden. So they hid from the LORD God among the trees. ⁹ Then the LORD God called to the man, "Where are you?" ¹⁰ He replied, "I heard you walking in the garden, so I hid. I was afraid because I was naked." ¹¹ "Who told you that you were naked?" the LORD God asked. "Have you eaten from the tree whose fruit I commanded you not to eat?" ¹² The man replied, "It was the woman you gave me who gave me the fruit, and I ate it." ¹³ Then the LORD God asked the woman, "What have you done?" "The serpent deceived me," she replied. "That's why I ate it."

¹⁴ Then the LORD God said to the serpent, "Because you have done this, you are cursed more than all animals, domestic and wild. You will crawl on your belly, groveling in the dust as long as you live. ¹⁵ And I will cause hostility between you and the woman, and between your offspring and her offspring. He will strike your head, and you will strike his heel."

¹⁶ Then he said to the woman, "I will sharpen the pain of your pregnancy, and in pain you will give birth. And you will desire to control your husband, but he will rule over you."

¹⁷ And to the man he said, "Since you listened to your wife and ate from the tree whose fruit I commanded you not to eat, the ground is cursed because of you. All your life you will struggle to scratch a living from it. ¹⁸ It will grow thorns and thistles for you, though you will eat of its grains. ¹⁹ By the sweat of your brow will you have food to eat until you return to the ground from which you were made. For you were made from dust, and to dust you will return."

²⁰ Then the man—Adam—named his wife Eve, because she would be the mother of all who live. ²¹ And the LORD God made clothing from animal skins for Adam and his wife.

²² Then the LORD God said, "Look, the human beings have become like us, knowing both good and evil. What if they reach out, take fruit from the tree of life, and eat it? Then they will live forever!" ²³ So the LORD God banished them from the Garden of Eden, and he sent Adam out to cultivate the ground from which he had been made. ²⁴ After sending them out, the LORD God stationed mighty cherubim to the east of the Garden of Eden. And he placed a flaming sword that flashed back and forth to guard the way to the tree of life. (Genesis 3:1–24, NLT)

QUESTION 1—NOTICE: What do you notice about this passage? What is interesting or what stands out to you? (List at least 1 and no more than 3 observations)

QUESTION 2—CONSIDER: What don't you understand? What questions do you have about this passage? (List at least 1 and no more than 3 questions; try to answer your questions by looking more closely at this passage)

QUESTION 3—OBEY: What should you do or what can you apply to your life from this passage?

Write a statement below of what you will do as a result of this Bible study today: (then share this with one another)

"I will… _____

_____

_____

_____

- ☐ CLOSE IN PRAYER
- ☐ **ADDITIONAL DISCUSSION POINTS & FAQS:**

How could Eve be talking to a serpent? Not sure how this worked. It seems incredibly strange to us that Eve could have been talking to a reptile, but she doesn't seem surprised by this so maybe animals communicated with humans before sin entered the world. It was not the serpent speaking that should have alarmed them. Rather, it was the fact that he was causing them to doubt God's instructions (Genesis 3:1), contradicting God (Genesis 3:4), and calling God's motives into question (Genesis 3:5). That should have been enough to cause both Eve and Adam to stop talking to the serpent.

What did the serpent say to challenge God's authority? Notice that he brought doubt to the mind of Eve about what God had said. The devil still does this today by tempting people to disbelieve God's word.

Who ate the fruit first? Eve ate first and so she might have been deceived, but when she offered the fruit to Adam, he intentionally ate and willfully disobeyed God.

What excuses did they give for their sin? Adam blamed Eve for his disobedience. Eve blamed the serpent. People often provide excuses, but excuses don't excuse people from the consequences of their sin.

What consequences did God describe as a result of their sin: for the serpent, for Eve, for Adam?

- God told the serpent that he would forever afterward crawl on the ground in the dirt (like a snake), and promised that a redeemer wouldbe born from the "seed of the woman" who would crush the serpent's head with His heel. This is a direct prophecy of God sending His Son into the world, born of a virgin, to defeat the power of sin and death.
- To Eve God proclaimed that women would now experience pain in childbirth (this is to represent that another sinner has been born into the world). God also predicted that there would be strife in marriage over a desire to control one another.
- To Adam God predicted that men would face serious challenges as they tried to farm the land. Work would no longer be a joy, but would include many difficulties.

Why did God kill animals to cover Adam and Eve? The penalty for sin was death, therefore to cover sin a life must be given and blood sacrificed. God was teaching this to Adam and Eve so they would know that a sacrifice must be made for their sin.

Why did God kick them out of the Garden of Eden? At first this sounds like God was angry and didn't want them to live in the luxury of the Garden any longer, but at closer examination we read that the purpose for sending them out of the Garden was so that they would be unable to eat of the "Tree of Life" and live forever in their fallen sinful condition.

☐ **ADDITIONAL HELPS AND TOOLS:**

- Use more than one Bible version (i.e. New Living Translation, English Standard Version; New International Version). By comparing different versions, often a question is answered.
- ESV Study Bible: the notes can help you understand various Bible issues and provide additional information.
- *Sacred Sixty-Six Bible Overview* by Pastor Gary

Session 2 — Exodus 20 — The 10 Commandments

- WORSHIP—READ THIS PASSAGE: WHAT DOES JESUS WANT TO DO? **Revelation 3:20 "Look! I stand at the door and knock. If you hear my voice and open the door, I will come in, and we will share a meal together as friends.**

- BEGIN BY PRAYING TOGETHER

- LIST A HIGHLIGHT FROM LAST WEEK & CHALLENGE YOU ARE FACING

Highlight	Challenge

- HOW DID YOU DO IN OBEYING YOUR "I WILL" STATEMENT FROM LAST SESSION?

- WHO SHOULD BE A PART OF THIS BIBLE STUDY?

NEW LESSON—Introduction: (read this introduction out loud)

Here is an overview of the organization of the Bible.

<u>Genesis, Exodus, Leviticus, Numbers, and Deuteronomy</u>: These books are called The Law and were written by Moses. They cover the time from creation through 1400BC when the children of Israel were poised to enter the Promised Land of Canaan—basically modern Israel. Moses formalized the way the people approached God in worship through a system of animal sacrifices.

<u>Joshua to Esther</u>: The next 12 books detail the history of Israel from entering the Promised Land under the leadership of Joshua until 400BC which coincides with the end of the Old Testament.

<u>Job, Psalms, Proverbs, Ecclesiastes and Song of Solomon</u>: These books were written in Hebrew poetry and give wisdom from God and praise to God.

<u>Isaiah, Jeremiah, Lamentations, Ezekiel, and Daniel</u>: These books are called the Major Prophets, not because what they said was more important, but because the books are more extensive. They cover a crucial time in Israel's history (700 to 500BC) when God was declaring both His consequences for their sin and His future salvation because of His love.

<u>Hosea to Malachi</u>: These 12 books are called the Minor Prophets and cover a period of time between 800BC and 400BC. Malachi was the last prophet in the Old Testament and declared that the next prophet would "prepare the way for the Lord's arrival on earth."

At the end of Genesis, the children of Israel had moved to Egypt. Approximately 400 years passed, and the Egyptians enslaved them. God sent Moses to Pharaoh to demand that he would release the Israelites from slavery so they could enter the Promised Land. During Pharaoh's refusal 10 different plagues afflicted the Egyptian people until the final plague, death of all the firstborn, caused him to release the Jews. The Israelites were saved from death through institution of the Passover. Moses led them into the wilderness and to Mt. Sinai where he received special instruction from God. We call this, The Ten Commandments. Let's turn to Exodus 20 and discover this together."

☐   READ EXODUS 20:1-17 OUT LOUD.

Then God gave the people all these instructions: ² "I am the LORD your God, who rescued you from the land of Egypt, the place of your slavery.

(1) "You must not have any other god but me.

(2) "You must not make for yourself an idol of any kind or an image of anything in the heavens or on the earth or in the sea. 5 You must not bow down to them or worship them, for I, the LORD your God, am a jealous God who will not tolerate your affection for any other gods. I lay the sins of the parents upon their children; the entire family is affected—even children in the third and fourth generations of those who reject me. 6 But I lavish unfailing love for a thousand generations on those who love me and obey my commands.

(3) "You must not misuse the name of the LORD your God. The LORD will not let you go unpunished if you misuse his name.

(4) "Remember to observe the Sabbath day by keeping it holy. 9 You have six days each week for your ordinary work, 10 but the seventh day is a Sabbath day of rest dedicated to the LORD your God. On that day no one in your household may do any work. This includes you, your sons and daughters, your male and female servants, your livestock, and any foreigners living among you. 11 For in six days the LORD made the heavens, the earth, the sea, and everything in them; but on the seventh day he rested. That is why the LORD blessed the Sabbath day and set it apart as holy.

(5) "Honor your father and mother. Then you will live a long, full life in the land the LORD your God is giving you.

(6) "You must not murder.

(7) "You must not commit adultery.

(8) "You must not steal.

(9) "You must not testify falsely against your neighbor.

(10)   "You must not covet your neighbor's house. You must not covet your neighbor's wife, male or female servant, ox or donkey, or anything else that belongs to your neighbor."

 *Use the questions below to discuss this Bible passage.*

1. What does this Scripture teach you about God?

2. What does it teach you about yourself, or about people in general?

3. Is there a sin to avoid or a command to obey? (pick one)

4. Is there a promise to believe or an example to follow?

5. What will you do as a result of this study in the Bible?

Write a statement below of what you will do as a result of this Bible study today:

"I will… _____
_____
_____
_____

☐ CLOSE IN PRAYER

Session 3 — Psalm 103 — God's Loving Character

- ☐ BEGIN BY PRAYING TOGETHER

- ☐ WORSHIP—COMPARE THESE 2 PASSAGES. HOW DOES GOD SEE DEATH?

    ***Ezekiel 33:11** I take no pleasure in the death of wicked people. I only want them to turn from their wicked ways so they can live.*

    ***Psalm 116:15 (NIV84)** Precious in the sight of the LORD is the death of his saints.*

- ☐ LIST A HIGHLIGHT FROM LAST WEEK & CHALLENGE YOU ARE FACING

    Highlight   Challenge

    _____   _____

    _____   _____

- ☐ HOW DID YOU DO IN OBEYING YOUR "I WILL" STATEMENT FROM LAST SESSION?

- ☐ WHO SHOULD BE A PART OF THIS BIBLE STUDY?

    _____   _____

    _____   _____

NEW LESSON—Introduction: (read this introduction out loud)

After the children of Israel entered the Promised Land they experienced a time of prosperity. This prosperity led them to forget to worship God and brought times of great struggle as God disciplined them for their disobedience.

God's appointed representatives led the nation until the people requested a king. God selected Saul as their first king and David as the second king (c. 1000BC). King David was called a man after God's own heart and he led the nation to follow the Lord. David wrote many songs (called Psalms) that praised God for His loving care for His people.

Today we will look at one of his songs of praise. There are many people who think God in the Old Testament is harsh and judgmental, while God in the New Testament is more loving and kind. So let's read this Psalm to better understand God's eternal character and nature.

<u>**Psalm 103**</u> *A psalm of David.*

Let all that I am praise the LORD; with my whole heart, I will praise his holy name. ² Let all that I am praise the LORD; may I never forget the good things he does for me. ³ He forgives all my sins and heals all my diseases. ⁴ He redeems me from death and crowns me with love

and tender mercies. ⁵ He fills my life with good things. My youth is renewed like the eagle's!

⁶ The LORD gives righteousness and justice to all who are treated unfairly. ⁷ He revealed his character to Moses and his deeds to the people of Israel. ⁸ The LORD is compassionate and merciful, slow to get angry and filled with unfailing love. ⁹ He will not constantly accuse us, nor remain angry forever. ¹⁰ He does not punish us for all our sins; he does not deal harshly with us, as we deserve. ¹¹ For his unfailing love toward those who fear him is as great as the height of the heavens above the earth. ¹² He has removed our sins as far from us as the east is from the west.

¹³ The LORD is like a father to his children, tender and compassionate to those who fear him. ¹⁴ For he knows how weak we are; he remembers we are only dust. ¹⁵ Our days on earth are like grass; like wildflowers, we bloom and die. ¹⁶ The wind blows, and we are gone— as though we had never been here. ¹⁷ But the love of the LORD remains forever with those who fear him. His salvation extends to the children's children ¹⁸ of those who are faithful to his covenant, of those who obey his commandments!

¹⁹ The LORD has made the heavens his throne; from there he rules over everything. ²⁰ Praise the LORD, you angels, you mighty ones who carry out his plans, listening for each of his commands. ²¹ Yes, praise the LORD, you armies of angels who serve him and do his will! ²² Praise the LORD, everything he has created, everything in all his kingdom. Let all that I am praise the LORD.

 Use the questions below to discuss this Bible passage.

QUESTION 1—NOTICE: What do you notice about this passage? What is interesting or what stands out to you? (List at least 1 and no more than 3 observations)

QUESTION 2—CONSIDER: What don't you understand? What questions do you have about this passage? (List at least 1 and no more than 3 questions; try to answer your questions by looking more closely at this passage)

QUESTION 3—OBEY: What should you do or what can you apply to your life from this passage?

Write a statement below of what you will do as a result of this Bible study today: (then share this with one another)

"I will... _____

_____

_____

_____

☐   **CLOSE IN PRAYER**

Session 4 — Isaiah 53 — Messiah Offered for Sin

☐ BEGIN BY PRAYING TOGETHER

☐ WORSHIP—CONTLATE THESE 2 PASSAGES
The moon and stars were the work of God's fingers:
Psalm 8:3 When I look at the night sky and see the work of your fingers—the moon and the stars you set in place

But God had to roll up His sleeves to provide our salvation: *Isaiah 52:10 (NIV84) The LORD will lay bare his holy arm in the sight of all the nations, and all the ends of the earth will see the salvation of our God.*

☐ BEGIN BY PRAYING TOGETHER

☐ LIST A HIGHLIGHT FROM LAST WEEK & CHALLENGE YOU ARE FACING

Highlight   Challenge

_____   _____

_____   _____

☐ HOW DID YOU DO IN OBEYING YOUR "I WILL" STATEMENT FROM LAST SESSION?

☐ WHO SHOULD BE A PART OF THIS BIBLE STUDY?

_____   _____

_____   _____

NEW LESSON—Introduction: (read this introduction out loud)

"Throughout the Old Testament God was moving toward the time when He would send a Redeemer into the world to provide the ultimate sacrifice for our sin. From immediately after the first sin (remember Genesis 3), when God promised this Redeemer, all of the sacrifices had been a representation of the coming Messiah. The Law, the books of history, the books of poetry and the prophets all looked forward to this future Savior. Jesus said, '*You search the Scriptures because you think they give you eternal life. But the Scriptures point to me!*' (John 5:39,NLT). To summarize the books of prophecy we can read Isaiah 53 written about 700 years before Christ."

Read this out loud…

Isaiah 53

¹ *Who has believed our message? To whom has the L*ORD *revealed his powerful arm?* ² *My servant grew up in the L*ORD*'s presence like a tender green shoot, like a root in dry ground. There was nothing beautiful or majestic about his appearance, nothing to attract us to him.* ³ *He was despised and rejected— a man of sorrows, acquainted with deepest grief. We turned our backs on him and looked the other way. He was despised, and we did not care.* ⁴ *Yet it was our weaknesses he carried; it was our sorrows that weighed him down. And we thought his troubles were a punishment from God, a punishment for his own sins!*

⁵ *But he was pierced for our rebellion, crushed for our sins. He was beaten so we could be whole. He was whipped so we could be healed.* ⁶ *All of us, like sheep, have strayed away. We have left God's paths to follow our own. Yet the L*ORD *laid on him the sins of us all.* ⁷ *He was oppressed and treated harshly, yet he never said a word. He was led like a lamb to the slaughter. And as a sheep is silent before the shearers, he did not open his mouth.*

⁸ *Unjustly condemned, he was led away. No one cared that he died without descendants, that his life was cut short in midstream. But he was struck down for the rebellion of my people.* ⁹ *He had done no wrong and had never deceived anyone. But he was buried like a criminal; he was put in a rich man's grave.* ¹⁰ *But it was the L*ORD*'s good plan to crush him and cause him grief. Yet when his life is made an offering for sin, he will have many descendants. He will enjoy a long life, and the L*ORD*'s good plan will prosper in his hands.* ¹

¹ *When he sees all that is accomplished by his anguish, he will be satisfied. And because of his experience, my righteous servant will make it possible for many to be counted righteous, for he will bear all their sins.* ¹² *I will give him the honors of a victorious soldier, because he exposed himself to death. He was counted among the rebels. He bore the sins of many and interceded for rebels.*

 Use the questions below to discuss this Bible passage.

1. What did you like about this passage?

2. What is something in the passage that bothered you or left you confused?

3. Based on this Scripture what can you observe is true about people?

4. Based on this passage what is true about God?

5. What do you need to do in response to this story?

Write an "I will" statement below to describe what you will do as a result of studying this Scripture today.

"I will… _____
_____
_____
_____

☐   CLOSE IN PRAYER

Session 5 — John 1 — God's Son Comes to Us

☐ BEGIN BY PRAYING TOGETHER

☐ WORSHIP—WHAT IS THE VALUE OF STUDYING THE BIBLE?
2 Timothy 3:16–17 All Scripture is inspired by God and is useful to teach us what is true and to make us realize what is wrong in our lives. It corrects us when we are wrong and teaches us to do what is right. ⁱ⁷ God uses it to prepare and equip his people to do every good work.

☐ LIST A HIGHLIGHT FROM LAST WEEK & CHALLENGE YOU ARE FACING

Highlight   Challenge

_____   _____

_____   _____

☐ HOW DID YOU DO IN OBEYING YOUR "I WILL" STATEMENT FROM LAST SESSION?

NEW LESSON—Introduction: (read this introduction out loud)

Today we come to the New Testament. The first four books are called Gospels. These are written to tell the story of Jesus for the purpose that people would believe in Him and have eternal life. Next is the book of Acts, which tells the story of the early church for about 30 years after Jesus was resurrected. Then there are 13 books or letters (Romans thru Philemon) written by the Apostle Paul to churches and people to encourage them how to live as Christians.

The next 8 letters were written by various writers to Christians everywhere—especially Jewish Christians who were scattered around the world because of persecution. The last book is Revelation and describes the end times and the return of Christ to establish His kingdom on earth.

For 400 years there had not been a prophet in Israel. God remained silent until it was time for Jesus to be born in Bethlehem to a virgin named Mary, and her fiancé, Joseph. Jesus is the single most influential person who has ever lived, yet he never traveled more than a few dozen miles from home. He didn't write any books or hold any political office. He only ministered for about 3 years and yet his legacy still impacts billions of people today—almost 2000 years later. How can this be? Today we will consider what the Bible says about him. Let's turn to John chapter 1.

John 1:1–34 (Read this out loud)
¹ In the beginning the Word already existed. The Word was with God, and the Word was God. ² He existed in the beginning with God. ³ God created everything through him, and nothing was created except

through him. *⁴ The Word gave life to everything that was created, and his life brought light to everyone. ⁵ The light shines in the darkness, and the darkness can never extinguish it. ⁶ God sent a man, John the Baptist, ⁷ to tell about the light so that everyone might believe because of his testimony.*

⁸ John himself was not the light; he was simply a witness to tell about the light. ⁹ The one who is the true light, who gives light to everyone, was coming into the world. ¹⁰ He came into the very world he created, but the world didn't recognize him. ¹¹ He came to his own people, and even they rejected him. ¹² But to all who believed him and accepted him, he gave the right to become children of God. ¹³ They are reborn— not with a physical birth resulting from human passion or plan, but a birth that comes from God. ¹

⁴ So the Word became human and made his home among us. He was full of unfailing love and faithfulness. And we have seen his glory, the glory of the Father's one and only Son. ¹⁵ John testified about him when he shouted to the crowds, "This is the one I was talking about when I said, 'Someone is coming after me who is far greater than I am, for he existed long before me.' "

¹⁶ From his abundance we have all received one gracious blessing after another. ¹⁷ For the law was given through Moses, but God's unfailing love and faithfulness came through Jesus Christ. ¹⁸ No one has ever seen God. But the unique One, who is himself God, is near to the Father's heart. He has revealed God to us. ¹⁹ This was John's testimony when the Jewish leaders sent priests and Temple assistants from Jerusalem to ask John, "Who are you?"

²⁰ He came right out and said, "I am not the Messiah." ²¹ "Well then, who are you?" they asked. "Are you Elijah?" "No," he replied. "Are you the Prophet we are expecting?" "No." ²² "Then who are you? We need an answer for those who sent us. What do you have to say about yourself?" ²³ John replied in the words of the prophet Isaiah: "I am a voice shouting in the wilderness, 'Clear the way for the LORD's coming!' " ²⁴ Then the Pharisees who had been sent ²⁵ asked him, "If you aren't the Messiah or Elijah or the Prophet, what right do you have to baptize?" ²⁶ John told them, "I baptize with water, but right here in the crowd is someone you do not recognize.

²⁷ Though his ministry follows mine, I'm not even worthy to be his slave and untie the straps of his sandal." ²⁸ This encounter took place in Bethany, an area east of the Jordan River, where John was baptizing. ²⁹ The next day John saw Jesus coming toward him and said, "Look! The Lamb of God who takes away the sin of the world! ³⁰ He is the one I was talking about when I said, 'A man is coming after me who is far greater than I am, for he existed long before me.'

³¹ I did not recognize him as the Messiah, but I have been baptizing with water so that he might be revealed to Israel." ³² Then John testified, "I saw the Holy Spirit descending like a dove from heaven and resting upon him. ³³ I didn't know he was the one, but when God sent me to baptize with water, he told me, 'The one on whom you see the Spirit descend and rest is the one who will baptize with the Holy Spirit.' ³⁴ I saw this happen to Jesus, so I testify that he is the Chosen One of God."

 Use the questions below to discuss this Bible passage.

QUESTION 1—NOTICE: What do you notice about this passage? What is interesting or what stands out to you? (List at least 1 and no more than 3 observations)

QUESTION 2—CONSIDER: What don't you understand? What questions do you have about this passage? (List at least 1 and no more than 3 questions; try to answer your questions by looking more closely at this passage)

QUESTION 3—OBEY: What should you do or what can you apply to your life from this passage?

Write a statement below of what you will do as a result of this Bible study today: (then share this with one another)

"I will... _____

_____

_____

_____

☐   CLOSE IN PRAYER

Session 6 — Matthew 28 — Jesus' Crucifixion & Resurrection

- ☐ BEGIN BY PRAYING TOGETHER

- ☐ WORSHIP—CONTEMPLATE THIS PASSAGE. What does God think of you?
  Psalm 139 O LORD, you have examined my heart and know everything about me...You know everything I do. ⁴ You know what I am going to say even before I say it, LORD...¹³ You made all the delicate, inner parts of my body and knit me together in my mother's womb. ¹⁴ Thank you for making me so wonderfully complex!... ¹⁷ How precious are your thoughts about me, O God. They cannot be numbered! ... ²³ Search me, O God, and know my heart; test me and know my anxious thoughts. ²⁴ Point out anything in me that offends you, and lead me along the path of everlasting life.

- ☐ LIST A HIGHLIGHT FROM LAST WEEK & CHALLENGE YOU ARE FACING

  Highlight   Challenge

  _____   _____

  _____   _____

- ☐ HOW DID YOU DO IN OBEYING YOUR "I WILL" STATEMENT FROM LAST SESSION?

NEW LESSON—Introduction: (read this introduction out loud)

Jesus began his ministry after he was baptized by John. He taught a new way of living in God's kingdom summarizing all the commandments with "love God with all your heart, soul, mind and strength, and love your neighbor as yourself." He performed many miracles: He walked on water, turned water into wine, fed 5000, healed the sick, cast out demons and even raised the dead. Even those who opposed him could not refute his miracles. But more importantly, he continually reminded people that his mission was to suffer and die for the sins of all people and then to rise from the dead. Today let's look at the most significant event in human history: the death and resurrection of Jesus Christ. At about 9 am they nailed Jesus to the cross. Let's pick up the story from there... Matthew 27:45.

Matthew 27:45–66
⁴⁵ At noon, darkness fell across the whole land until three o'clock. ⁴⁶ At about three o'clock, Jesus called out with a loud voice, "Eli, Eli, lema sabachthani?" which means "My God, my God, why have you abandoned me?" ⁴⁷ Some of the bystanders misunderstood and thought he was calling for the prophet Elijah.

⁴⁸ One of them ran and filled a sponge with sour wine, holding it up to him on a reed stick so he could drink. ⁴⁹ But the rest said, "Wait! Let's see whether Elijah comes to save him." ⁵⁰ Then Jesus shouted out again, and he released his spirit. ⁵¹ At that moment the curtain in the sanctuary of the Temple was torn in two, from top to bottom. The earth shook, rocks split apart, ⁵² and tombs opened. The bodies of many godly men and women who had died were raised from the dead. ⁵³ They left the cemetery after Jesus' resurrection, went into the holy city of Jerusalem, and appeared to many people.

⁵⁴ The Roman officer and the other soldiers at the crucifixion were terrified by the earthquake and all that had happened. They said, "This man truly was the Son of God!" ⁵⁵ And many women who had come from Galilee with Jesus to care for him were watching from a distance. ⁵⁶ Among them were Mary Magdalene, Mary (the mother of James and Joseph), and the mother of James and John, the sons of Zebedee.

⁵⁷ As evening approached, Joseph, a rich man from Arimathea who had become a follower of Jesus, ⁵⁸ went to Pilate and asked for Jesus' body. And Pilate issued an order to release it to him. ⁵⁹ Joseph took the body and wrapped it in a long sheet of clean linen cloth. ⁶⁰ He placed it in his own new tomb, which had been carved out of the rock. Then he rolled a great stone across the entrance and left. ⁶¹ Both Mary Magdalene and the other Mary were sitting across from the tomb and watching. ⁶² The next day, on the Sabbath, the leading priests and Pharisees went to see Pilate.

⁶³ They told him, "Sir, we remember what that deceiver once said while he was still alive: 'After three days I will rise from the dead.' ⁶⁴ So we request that you seal the tomb until the third day. This will prevent his disciples from coming and stealing his body and then telling everyone he was raised from the dead! If that happens, we'll be worse off than we were at first." ⁶⁵ Pilate replied, "Take guards and secure it the best you can." ⁶⁶ So they sealed the tomb and posted guards to protect it.

Matthew 28:1-20
¹ Early on Sunday morning, as the new day was dawning, Mary Magdalene and the other Mary went out to visit the tomb. ² Suddenly there was a great earthquake! For an angel of the Lord came down from heaven, rolled aside the stone, and sat on it. ³ His face shone like lightning, and his clothing was as white as snow. ⁴ The guards shook with fear when they saw him, and they fell into a dead faint.

⁵ Then the angel spoke to the women. "Don't be afraid!" he said. "I know you are looking for Jesus, who was crucified. ⁶ He isn't here! He is risen from the dead, just as he said would happen. Come, see where his body was lying.

7 *And now, go quickly and tell his disciples that he has risen from the dead, and he is going ahead of you to Galilee. You will see him there. Remember what I have told you."* **8** *The women ran quickly from the tomb. They were very frightened but also filled with great joy, and they rushed to give the disciples the angel's message.*

9 *And as they went, Jesus met them and greeted them. And they ran to him, grasped his feet, and worshiped him.* **10** *Then Jesus said to them, "Don't be afraid! Go tell my brothers to leave for Galilee, and they will see me there."* **11** *As the women were on their way, some of the guards went into the city and told the leading priests what had happened.* **12** *A meeting with the elders was called, and they decided to give the soldiers a large bribe.*

13 *They told the soldiers, "You must say, 'Jesus' disciples came during the night while we were sleeping, and they stole his body.'* **14** *If the governor hears about it, we'll stand up for you so you won't get in trouble."* **15** *So the guards accepted the bribe and said what they were told to say. Their story spread widely among the Jews, and they still tell it today.* **16** *Then the eleven disciples left for Galilee, going to the mountain where Jesus had told them to go.*

17 *When they saw him, they worshiped him—but some of them doubted!* **18** *Jesus came and told his disciples, "I have been given all authority in heaven and on earth.* **19** *Therefore, go and make disciples of all the nations, baptizing them in the name of the Father and the Son and the Holy Spirit.* **20** *Teach these new disciples to obey all the commands I have given you. And be sure of this: I am with you always, even to the end of the age."*

 Use the questions below to discuss this Bible passage.

1. What did you like about this story?

2. What is something in the story that bothered you or left you confused?

3. Based on this Scripture what can you observe is true about people?

4. Based on this story what is true about God?

5. What do you need to do in response to this story?

Write an "I will" statement below to describe what you will do as a result of studying this Scripture today.

"I will… _____
_____
_____
_____

☐ CLOSE IN PRAYER

Session 7 — Romans 8 — Victorious Christian Living

- ☐ BEGIN BY PRAYING TOGETHER

- ☐ WORSHIP—CONTEMPLATE THIS PASSAGE. What does it meant to "trust i the Lord?"

   Isaiah 40:31 But those who trust in the LORD will find new strength. They will soar high on wings like eagles. They will run and not grow weary. They will walk and not faint.

- ☐ LIST A HIGHLIGHT FROM LAST WEEK & CHALLENGE YOU ARE FACING

Highlight	Challenge

- ☐ HOW DID YOU DO IN OBEYING YOUR "I WILL" STATEMENT FROM LAST SESSION?

New Lesson— Introduction: (read out loud)

After Jesus raised from the dead he showed himself to hundreds of people over a period of 40 days. Then he was taken into heaven and promised to return. Ten days later, the church began as Peter preached about Jesus' death and resurrection. The message of the good news about God's salvation through Jesus was proclaimed throughout the known world. Tens of thousands of people responded by becoming followers of Christ. One of the important leaders of the church was a former Jewish leader who became the Apostle Paul.

He wrote many important letters to the Christians in churches all over the world. One of the great letters he wrote was the book of Romans. Chapter 8 of this book is one of the most important passages in the Bible. It describes how a follower of Jesus can live a victorious life through God's power.

LIFE IN THE SPIRIT

Romans 8
¹ So now there is no condemnation for those who belong to Christ Jesus. ² And because you belong to him, the power of the life-giving Spirit has freed you from the power of sin that leads to death. ³ The law of Moses was unable to save us because of the weakness of our sinful nature. So God did what the law could not do. He sent his own Son in a body like the bodies we sinners have. And in that body God declared an end to sin's control over us by giving his Son as a sacrifice for our sins.

⁴ He did this so that the just requirement of the law would be fully satisfied for us, who no longer follow our sinful nature but instead follow the Spirit. ⁵ Those who are dominated by the sinful nature think about sinful things, but those who are controlled by the Holy Spirit think about things that please the Spirit. ⁶ So letting your sinful nature control your mind leads to death. But letting the Spirit control your mind leads to life and peace.

⁷ For the sinful nature is always hostile to God. It never did obey God's laws, and it never will. ⁸ That's why those who are still under the control of their sinful nature can never please God. ⁹ But you are not controlled by your sinful nature. You are controlled by the Spirit if you have the Spirit of God living in you. (And remember that those who do not have the Spirit of Christ living in them do not belong to him at all.) ¹⁰ And Christ lives within you, so even though your body will die because of sin, the Spirit gives you life because you have been made right with God.

¹¹ The Spirit of God, who raised Jesus from the dead, lives in you. And just as God raised Christ Jesus from the dead, he will give life to your mortal bodies by this same Spirit living within you. ¹² Therefore, dear brothers and sisters, you have no obligation to do what your sinful nature urges you to do. ¹³ For if you live by its dictates, you will die. But if through the power of the Spirit you put to death the deeds of your sinful nature, you will live. ¹⁴ For all who are led by the Spirit of God are children of God.

¹⁵ So you have not received a spirit that makes you fearful slaves. Instead, you received God's Spirit when he adopted you as his own children. Now we call him, "Abba, Father." ¹⁶ For his Spirit joins with our spirit to affirm that we are God's children. ¹⁷ And since we are his children, we are his heirs. In fact, together with Christ we are heirs of God's glory. But if we are to share his glory, we must also share his suffering.

FUTURE GLORY

¹⁸ Yet what we suffer now is nothing compared to the glory he will reveal to us later. ¹⁹ For all creation is waiting eagerly for that future day when God will reveal who his children really are. ²⁰ Against its will, all creation was subjected to God's curse. But with eager hope, ²¹ the creation looks forward to the day when it will join God's children in glorious freedom from death and decay. ²² For we know that all creation has been groaning as in the pains of childbirth right up to the present time. ²³ And we believers also groan, even though we have the Holy Spirit within us as a foretaste of future glory, for we long for our bodies to be released from sin and suffering. We, too, wait with eager hope for the day when God will give us our full rights as his adopted children, including the new bodies he has promised us.

²⁴ We were given this hope when we were saved. (If we already have something, we don't need to hope for it. ²⁵ But if we look forward to something we don't yet have, we must wait patiently and confidently.) ²⁶ And the Holy Spirit helps us in our weakness.

For example, we don't know what God wants us to pray for. But the Holy Spirit prays for us with groanings that cannot be expressed in words. ²⁷ And the Father who knows all hearts knows what the Spirit is saying, for the Spirit pleads for us believers in harmony with God's own will.

More Than Conquerors
²⁸ And we know that God causes everything to work together for the good of those who love God and are called according to his purpose for them. ²⁹ For God knew his people in advance, and he chose them to become like his Son, so that his Son would be the firstborn among many brothers and sisters. ³⁰ And having chosen them, he called them to come to him. And having called them, he gave them right standing with himself. And having given them right standing, he gave them his glory. ³¹ What shall we say about such wonderful things as these? If God is for us, who can ever be against us?

³² Since he did not spare even his own Son but gave him up for us all, won't he also give us everything else? ³³ Who dares accuse us whom God has chosen for his own? No one—for God himself has given us right standing with himself. ³⁴ Who then will condemn us? No one— for Christ Jesus died for us and was raised to life for us, and he is sitting in the place of honor at God's right hand, pleading for us. ³⁵ Can anything ever separate us from Christ's love? Does it mean he no longer loves us if we have trouble or calamity, or are persecuted, or hungry, or destitute, or in danger, or threatened with death?

³⁶ (As the Scriptures say, "For your sake we are killed every day; we are being slaughtered like sheep.") ³⁷ No, despite all these things, overwhelming victory is ours through Christ, who loved us. ³⁸ And I am convinced that nothing can ever separate us from God's love. Neither death nor life, neither angels nor demons, neither our fears for today nor our worries about tomorrow—not even the powers of hell can separate us from God's love. ³⁹ No power in the sky above or in the earth below—indeed, nothing in all creation will ever be able to separate us from the love of God that is revealed in Christ Jesus our Lord.

 Use the questions below to discuss this Bible passage.

QUESTION 1—NOTICE: What do you notice about this passage? What is interesting or what stands out to you? (List at least 1 and no more than 3 observations)

QUESTION 2—CONSIDER: What don't you understand? What questions do you have about this passage? (List at least 1 and no more than 3 questions; try to answer your questions by looking more closely at this passage)

QUESTION 3—OBEY: What should you do or what can you apply to your life from this passage?

Write a statement below of what you will do as a result of this Bible study today: (then share this with one another)

"I will… _____

_____

_____

_____

☐   CLOSE IN PRAYER

Session 8 — Revelation 20 — Jesus Returns to Rule

- ☐ BEGIN BY PRAYING TOGETHER

- ☐ WORSHIP—READ THROUGH THESE HIGHLIGHT VERSES FROM THE PREVIOUS CHAPTERS WE HAVE STUDIED.

    Exodus 20:6 But I lavish unfailing love for a thousand generations on those who love me and obey my commands.

    Psalm 103:13 The LORD is like a father to his children, tender and compassionate to those who fear him.

    Isaiah 53:6 All of us, like sheep, have strayed away. We have left God's paths to follow our own. Yet the LORD laid on him the sins of us all.

    John 1:29 The next day John saw Jesus coming toward him and said, "Look! The Lamb of God who takes away the sin of the world!

    Matthew 28:5–6a Then the angel spoke to the women...He isn't here! He is risen from the dead!

    Romans 8:31b If God is for us, who can ever be against us?

- ☐ LIST A HIGHLIGHT FROM LAST WEEK & CHALLENGE YOU ARE FACING

Highlight	Challenge

- ☐ HOW DID YOU DO IN OBEYING YOUR "I WILL" STATEMENT FROM LAST SESSION?

NEW LESSON—Introduction: (read this out loud)
As people heard the good news about eternal life through faith in Jesus, tens of thousands believed and were gathered into churches all over the known world. Many of the books of the New Testament provide guidance for Christian living. But when Jesus was taken into heaven, he promised to return again and establish His kingdom on earth. His return means that the world will experience peace and justice and His benevolent rule as King of kings. There are many events that will happen but will culminate with Jesus' return. We can read about this in Revelation 20."

Revelation 20
1 Then I saw an angel coming down from heaven with the key to the bottomless pit and a heavy chain in his hand. ² He seized the dragon—that old serpent, who is the devil, Satan—and bound him in chains for a thousand years. ³ The angel threw him into the bottomless pit, which he then shut and locked so Satan could not deceive the nations anymore until the thousand years were finished.

Afterward he must be released for a little while. ⁴ *Then I saw thrones, and the people sitting on them had been given the authority to judge. And I saw the souls of those who had been beheaded for their testimony about Jesus and for proclaiming the word of God. They had not worshiped the beast or his statue, nor accepted his mark on their forehead or their hands. They all came to life again, and they reigned with Christ for a thousand years.*

⁵ *This is the first resurrection. (The rest of the dead did not come back to life until the thousand years had ended.)* ⁶ *Blessed and holy are those who share in the first resurrection. For them the second death holds no power, but they will be priests of God and of Christ and will reign with him a thousand years.* ⁷ *When the thousand years come to an end, Satan will be let out of his prison.* ⁸ *He will go out to deceive the nations—called Gog and Magog—in every corner of the earth. He will gather them together for battle—a mighty army, as numberless as sand along the seashore.*

⁹ *And I saw them as they went up on the broad plain of the earth and surrounded God's people and the beloved city. But fire from heaven came down on the attacking armies and consumed them.* ¹⁰ *Then the devil, who had deceived them, was thrown into the fiery lake of burning sulfur, joining the beast and the false prophet. There they will be tormented day and night forever and ever.*

¹¹ *And I saw a great white throne and the one sitting on it. The earth and sky fled from his presence, but they found no place to hide.* ¹² *I saw the dead, both great and small, standing before God's throne. And the books were opened, including the Book of Life. And the dead were judged according to what they had done, as recorded in the books.* ¹³ *The sea gave up its dead, and death and the grave gave up their dead. And all were judged according to their deeds.* ¹⁴ *Then death and the grave were thrown into the lake of fire. This lake of fire is the second death.* ¹⁵ *And anyone whose name was not found recorded in the Book of Life was thrown into the lake of fire.*

 Use the questions below to discuss this Bible passage.

1. What does this Scripture teach you about God?

2. What does it teach you about yourself, or about people in general?

3. Is there a sin to avoid or a command to obey? (pick one)

4. Is there a promise to believe or an example to follow?

5. What will you do as a result of this study in the Bible?

Write a statement below of what you will do as a result of this Bible study today:

"I will… _____

_____

_____

_____

☐ CLOSE IN PRAYER

Next Steps

The Discipleship Journey is Step 1 in the TCN Discipleship Process. This 8-session study is designed to introduce someone to the basic disciplines of following Jesus.

1. Assurance of Salvation
2. Baptism
3. Prayer
4. Bible Study & Devotions
5. Your Faith Story
6. God's Story—The Bridge
7. Church Christian Community
8. Practice Being the Church

 To order more *Thru the Bible,* or other TCN resources, contact us at…

Transforming Churches Network
1736 Edgeburg Lane | Cordova, TN 38016
901-494-7375
www.tcnprocess.com
terry@transformingchurchesnetwork.org

The Gospel of Mark is Step 3 in the TCN Discipleship Process.

The next few pages conatin an outline of 8 lessons with additional discussion questions.

GOSPEL OF MARK—Discovery Bible Study in 8 Lessons

Lesson	Scripture Passage	Additional Discussion Questions
1	**Mark 1:1-15** Jesus Baptized	1. How does Mark show us that Jesus is worthy of attention? 2. What "witnesses" does Mark call upon to introduce Jesus, and why? 3. What is meant by "repent," "believe," and "baptized?" 4. What implications does Jesus' experience of temptation have for the temptations we face? 5. What steps could you take this week to encourage other Christians to be better witnesses for Christ?

2	**Mark 2:1-12** Jesus Heals Paralyzed Man	1. What do the details of this story tell you about the paralytic man, his friends, and Jesus' reputation?
		2. If someone in a crowd of people said to you, "Your sins are forgiven", what would you and everyone else think of that person?
		3. How does Jesus demonstrate his claim to be able to forgive sin?
		4. Which is easier for you to do—forgive others or care for them when they are sick?
		5. Following the example of the paralytic man's friends, how could you go out of your way this week to help another believer who is experiencing pain or suffering?

3	**Mark 3:7-35** Jesus chooses Disciples & sends them out; answers critics	1. What was unusual about the crowds that came to see Jesus?
		2. What responses to Jesus do you see in this passage?
		3. Why was Jesus' authoritative teaching a threat to the teachers of the law?
		4. When, if ever, have you been thought of as "out of your mind" by other people because of your efforts to live a Christian life?
		5. According to this passage, how do you become a part of Jesus' family
		6. What can you do this week that will restore a relationship that strains your unity with other Christians?

4	**Mark 8:22-38** Jesus heals blind man; identifies himself	1. What event takes place just before Peter's confession? Why do you think these two stories are placed next to each other?
		2. What do we learn about Jesus' character from the way He treated the blind man?
		3. What did Jesus tell his disciples to do if they wanted to follow Him?
		4. According to Jesus, why does a follower of Christ have to "deny himself" and "lose his life"?
		5. What specific steps can you take to listen closely to Christ this week?

5	**Mark 10:17-45** Jesus & Rich Man	1. According to verses 17-22, what would Jesus say is the basic character of people in the world today?
		2. How did Jesus explain the way to inherit eternal life?
		3. In verses 32-34, Jesus says that he is going to die. According to verse 45, what is the purpose of his death?
		4. Read Isaiah 53:5, 10-12. How do these verses help us understand what a ransom is?
		5. What is one distraction you can set aside this week to help you concentrate more on devotion to Christ?

6	**Mark 14:53-15:15** Jesus' Arrest & Trial	1. Why did the Sanhedrin have such a difficult time convicting Jesus?
		2. How are some of the characters in this passage similar to each other? How are they different?
		3. What evidence is Mark presenting in his attempt to prove that Jesus is the Christ, the Son of God?
		4. How does Jesus' silence actually communicate his identity? (See Isaiah 53:7-9)
		5. What is one step you can take this week to strengthen your conviction against pressure from co-workers, family or friends?

7	**Mark 15:16-39** Jesus Crucified	1. How many times does the phrase "King of the Jews" appear in Chapter 15? What is ironic about this? What is Mark trying to say about the events at the cross?
		2. Read Psalm 22. How does this help you understand the words of Jesus from the cross in verse 34?
		3. How does Psalm 22 end? What is Jesus ultimately claiming for himself?
		4. Why do you think the events at the cross were necessary?
		5. What final description of Jesus' identity does Mark provide? Where have you seen this title before?
		6. What should be your response if you are criticized for your faith this week?
8	**Mark 15:42-16:8** Jesus Raised from Dead	1. Of what fact does Mark want his readers to be sure of in verses 42-47?
		2. What does Mark say happened to Jesus' body?
		3. What do Joseph's actions tell us about his own understanding of Jesus?
		4. Why is it significant that Jesus rose from the dead?
		5. What do you see as your personal role in helping spread the news about Christ?

www.ingramcontent.com/pod-product-compliance
Lightning Source LLC
Chambersburg PA
CBHW061348040426
42444CB00011B/3137